The Discovery Books are prepared

under the educational supervision of

Mary C. Austin, Ed.D.

Reading Specialist and

Professor of Education

Western Reserve University

# A DISCOVERY BOOK

**GARRARD PUBLISHING COMPANY**
CHAMPAIGN, ILLINOIS

# Franklin D. Roosevelt

## Four Times President

*by Wyatt Blassingame*

*illustrated by Al Fiorentino*

# Contents

## Franklin D. Roosevelt: Four Times President

# Chapter 1

# A Ship in a Tree

The tree's branches came close to the ground. Franklin Roosevelt, age seven, climbed up the tree carrying a rope. From the top he let down one end of the rope. His friend, Edmund Rogers, tied this to a long plank. Franklin pulled the plank up into the tree and carefully nailed it between two limbs. He let the rope down for another plank, then another.

While the boys were working, James Roosevelt, Franklin's father, rode up on a horse. He had been inspecting the farms on his estate. He stopped his horse under the tree. "That's a good tree-house you are building," he said.

Franklin stopped his hammering. "It's not a tree-house."

"No? What is it?"

"It's a ship."

Edmund Rogers, who was standing beside Mr. Roosevelt's horse, thought the big man would laugh. But Franklin knew his father never laughed at him. He might laugh with him at a joke, but he never laughed at him.

"A ship," Mr. Roosevelt said. "I can see that now. Where are you and Edmund sailing?"

"To China, like Mama did when she was a girl."

"Have a good voyage," Mr. Roosevelt said. "And be back in time for dinner."

Mr. Roosevelt rode off. Edmund climbed the tree to join Franklin in their ship. All the land and houses and the stables and barns they could see from their ship belonged to Franklin's wealthy father. The servants and hired farmers were going about their work. Off to the right was the big frame house where Franklin had been born in 1882. Beyond it was the Hudson River. This big Roosevelt estate was called Hyde Park. Here Franklin spent most of his childhood. Sometimes it was lonely. There were no brothers and sisters to play with, and few neighbors.

Franklin did not even go to school as most children did. His mother Sara liked to keep him close beside her. Sometimes she taught his lessons. She also hired private teachers who came to Hyde Park.

Yet Franklin was never very lonely. He had his own pony. He had a small shotgun, and he learned to mount the birds he killed. Soon he had a large collection of birds and bird eggs.

He also collected postage stamps. To start, his mother gave him a collection she had owned as a girl. Franklin loved the small, bright pictures. When he was nine he wrote to an aunt visiting abroad: *"Please tell Uncle Will that if he has any foreign stamps I should like to have them."*

Franklin himself traveled a great deal. He had many small cousins and often visited them. Several times he went to Europe with his father and mother. But he liked best to go to Campobello in the summers. This was a rocky, wooded Canadian island near the Maine coast. Here Franklin's father had a large sailboat. As Franklin got older he was given a small sailboat of his own. He loved to go skimming over the coves and inlets, his little boat leaning far over before the wind. All his life he would like ships and the sea.

When he was fourteen years old his life changed. His parents decided it would be good for him to go away to school. The school was called Groton.

# Chapter 2

# Runaway to War—Almost

At home Franklin had been an only child, the center of attention. At Groton he was just one boy among many. At home he had a large room with every comfort he could ask for. At school he lived in the dormitory. The room was small and bare. He had to get up at a certain time, go to classes on time, go to bed on time. It was a very different life.

Franklin loved it. He liked living with other boys. In turn, they liked him. He was a tall, handsome boy with blue eyes and fair hair. He took part in all the school activities. He went out for baseball, football, crew and boxing. He never made the first team, but he loved sports. One proud day he wrote:

*"Dear Papa and Mama*

*Last Monday was a red letter day for me; in the morning after school we had the . . . High Kick. There were about 15 Entries. . . . A tin pan was suspended from the ceiling of the Gym, about 3½ feet from the floor at first. As it rose the contestants dropped out one by one until I found myself one of the only three left."*

The other boys kicked as high as they could but could not reach the pan.

Each boy had three tries. Franklin missed twice. Then his third kick touched the pan. He won first prize.

During Franklin's first year at Groton most of his grades were just one mark above failing. Once he wrote his family:

*"I forgot to mention in my last letter, that I, together with many others had had the great pleasure of failing the most outrageous Greek exam. which has ever been known in the history of education. Not only was the paper unfair but the marking was atrocious, and altho' I got about .50 the old idiot Abbott refused to pass me as is customary when one almost passes."*

16

But Franklin did not give up. He added:

*"I take my Greek exam again next Saturday & I am working hard for it."*

This time he passed with a high mark.

Franklin's other marks improved also. Soon he was making a B average.

He enjoyed making speeches and did very well in debating. Franklin worked hard to know what to say and to say it properly. He practiced speaking clearly so each word could be understood. He tried to make his speeches sound as if he were talking in a personal way to his audience.

In 1898, Franklin's second year at Groton, the Spanish-American War began.

All the Groton boys were very excited.

Franklin had a famous cousin named Theodore Roosevelt. "Teddy" was much older than Franklin. He had been a politician in New York and a cowboy in the west. Now he was Assistant Secretary of the Navy. He left this post to start a troop of cavalry called the Rough Riders. Often Franklin read in the papers about his Cousin Teddy and the Rough Riders fighting in Cuba. It sounded exciting and dangerous.

One day Franklin told his friend Lathrop Brown, "I don't want my cousin to be the only Roosevelt in this war. I am going to run away from school and join the Navy."

"You aren't old enough," Lathrop said.

"I'll tell them I am eighteen."

"All right," his friend said. "I'll go with you."

How were they to slip away from school? "We'll get the man who sells pies to the school to take us," Franklin said. "We can pay him to hide us in his wagon. Nobody will miss us until it is too late."

The pieman agreed. Once away from school, the boys would need to take a train to Boston. They did not have enough money to do this. For weeks they saved their allowances. Finally their plans were all set. They would go in the pieman's wagon the next day.

That night Franklin thought it was excitement that made him feel strange. His head hurt. His stomach hurt.

Suddenly he was very sick. He was taken to the school hospital. "You have scarlet fever," the doctor told Franklin. "You will have to stay quietly in bed for a while."

By the time Franklin was well it was too late to go to the war.

# Chapter *3*

# First Election

After Groton, Franklin went to Harvard College. There he went out for football, baseball and crew. Again he did not make the varsity, but this did not bother him.

Franklin wanted most to be on the staff of the college paper, the *Crimson*. He got an interview with the President of the college. No one else had been able to do this. He got a story from his Cousin Theodore who was now President of the United States. It was not long before Franklin was a regular staff member of the paper. In his senior year he was the editor.

Franklin had a fifth cousin named Eleanor Roosevelt. She was a tall, graceful girl. She was not pretty, but she was sweet and charming. She looked beautiful to Franklin. In March, 1905, the year after he finished college, he and Eleanor were married.

Franklin's cousin, Theodore Roosevelt, was Eleanor's uncle. Because her father was dead, Uncle Teddy gave the bride away.

After the wedding Franklin and Eleanor stood in the reception line to greet their guests. But all the guests wanted to meet the President. Everybody crowded around him. The new bride and groom were forgotten.

Eleanor looked at her husband and laughed. "We might as well join the others. Nobody is ever going to take the spotlight from Uncle Teddy."

After his marriage Franklin studied law. He became a lawyer in New York City. He and Eleanor had a daughter named Anna, then a son named James. Franklin enjoyed playing with his children. He liked to take them sailing at Campobello and to Hyde Park to play under the trees.

One day some men came to see Franklin. They wanted him to run for the State Senate. If elected, he would represent the area around Hyde Park.

Franklin was a Democrat. Only once in more than 50 years had a Democrat been elected from this district. Nobody believed a Democrat could win now. But they needed someone to try. "Let me think about it," Franklin said.

He went home to talk it over with Eleanor. "You will have to make your own decision," she said. "But you have always been interested in politics."

This was true. Franklin wanted to follow in the footsteps of his famous cousin. He wanted to be President. "My Cousin Teddy started in the state government," Franklin said. "I'll run!"

His acceptance speech was short. "We have only one month before the election," he said. "It's going to be a very busy month."

This was 1910. There were only a few automobiles in the whole United States. There was just one in the district where Franklin was going to campaign. It was painted a bright red. Franklin hired it. Then he set out to meet the voters in his district.

"Now Franklin has lost any chance to win," some people said. "That automobile will frighten the farmers' horses and kill their chickens. It will not win him votes."

"My district is too big to cover in a horse and buggy," Franklin said. "I want to meet all the people possible, and time is short."

Day after day Franklin drove around the country. If his automobile frightened a horse, Franklin would stop and help.

This gave him a chance to talk politics with farmers. He talked to the people in small towns, on street corners, in stores. People liked the friendly way he smiled. They liked his loud, easy laugh. They felt sure he would work to help them.

When the votes were counted Franklin and Eleanor were tense with excitement. Even little Anna and James were excited. The race was so close that at first nobody was sure who had won.

Finally all the votes were counted. Franklin had won his first political victory.

# Chapter 4

# World War I

Franklin was a good State Senator. In 1912 he was elected a second time.

That same year Woodrow Wilson was elected President of the United States. Both he and Franklin were Democrats. After the election Franklin went to Washington to call on the President. He met Josephus Daniels, who was the new Secretary of the Navy.

"Franklin," Secretary Daniels said, "how would you like to be Assistant Secretary of the Navy?"

Frank was too excited to answer. He had always loved ships and the sea. Besides, his Cousin Teddy had once held this job. "I'd like it better than anything in the world!" he said.

Franklin worked hard at this job just as he had worked hard at being State Senator. In August, 1914, World War I began. The United States was not in the war at the start. But American merchant ships carried supplies to the British and French. German submarines soon began to sink these ships. Many Americans became very angry at the Germans. In April, 1917, the United States declared war on Germany.

Now Franklin had more important work than ever. He had to rush from one navy yard to another. The United States was now building more ships to fight in the war. Franklin's office desk was always piled high with important papers. There were many great decisions for him to make. Franklin loved his work. He always enjoyed doing a big job in a big way.

He and Eleanor had five children now. Anna was eleven and James ten. Then there were Elliot, seven; Franklin, Jr., three; and the baby, John.

Sometimes Franklin took the children with him to inspect the navy yards. Sailors showed his small sons around the big ships. They enjoyed it as much as Franklin.

Although Franklin liked his work, there was something he wanted still more. As Assistant Secretary of the Navy his job did not take him into the actual fighting. Franklin tried to resign his job and join the Navy.

Josephus Daniels would not let him leave. "You are needed where you are," he said, "for the good of your country."

Finally Franklin persuaded Secretary Daniels to send him to Europe. He was to find more ways for the American navy to work with the navies of other countries. He visited American Marines in the front lines. He saw wounded and dying men. It was an experience he would never forget, though the war was soon over.

*Chapter* 5

# Polio!

In 1920 the Democratic Party named Franklin Roosevelt to run for Vice-President of the United States. Franklin campaigned hard, the way he did everything. He traveled thousands of miles throughout the country and made hundreds of speeches. When the election was over, the Republicans had won.

"The campaign was good for me, even if we lost," Franklin told his wife.

"It took me to every state in the Union. I made many friends. These will all be helpful, if I ever run again for national office."

Eleanor knew about his dream of being President. "You will run again," she said.

Then, without warning, something happened that changed his whole life.

It was August, 1921. Franklin had taken his family to Campobello for a vacation. One day he and Anna and James and Elliot were out sailing. A good breeze was blowing. The boat raced through the water.

Suddenly James, who was thirteen, shouted, "Look! A forest fire!"

From a nearby island smoke rose high into the sky. Quickly Roosevelt steered the boat to land. He and the children jumped out to fight the fire. It was hot, hard work. When at last the fire was out they sailed back to Campobello.

"There is just one way to get all this smoke and grime off us," Franklin told his children. He ran to a cove and dived into the icy water. Shouting with laughter, the children followed. After the swim they all walked back home. Franklin sat down to read his mail without changing his wet bathing suit.

All at once he became cold. This changed to a fever. He went to bed. "There is no need to call a doctor," he told Eleanor. "I'll soon be all right."

Next day he was worse. His legs and back hurt. Eleanor called a doctor who said, "It's a cold. He will get well."

Next day Franklin could not move his legs. The pain was terrible. A specialist came to see him. Still, days passed before anyone could be sure what was wrong.

Franklin Roosevelt had polio!

He was 39 years old. He had been strong and healthy. He had always loved the outdoors. He had loved to sail and swim, play golf and tennis, roll and tumble on the lawn with his children. Now he could not move his legs. He could barely move his hands and arms. He might not ever be able to move again.

Roosevelt had a close friend named Louis Howe. He was a small, ugly man who loved Franklin as a brother. Louis believed that one day Franklin would be President. He came to see Franklin and stood beside his bed. "You'll get well!" he said.

Because of the pain, Franklin could not even answer.

Howe turned and went out of the room. There were tears in his eyes. In the hall he told Eleanor, "He always seemed to me like the prince in a fairy story. He was young and handsome and rich. It seemed he could have anything he wanted. Now . . ."

"He will get well," Eleanor said. "We will make him get well." But she was afraid.

# Chapter *6*

# The Fight to Get Well

Weeks passed before Franklin could even be moved to a hospital. Then there were more pain-filled weeks when everything seemed to be hopeless. Slowly, however, Franklin began to regain his spirit. "If I am going to get well," he thought, "I have got to help myself. I will make myself get well. I will!"

Day after day he worked at the exercises the doctors had given him.

Slowly he regained the use of his hands and arms. He still could not move his legs, but he kept trying.

Finally he could leave the hospital. Later he and Eleanor went to Florida. They lived on a houseboat. Franklin could fish whenever he wished. This was good exercise for his arms, and it was fun, too.

One day he had Eleanor take him to the beach in his wheelchair. "Now watch me," he said. With her help he lifted himself out of the chair. Slowly he began to crawl along the beach, trying to force his legs to work. He lay at the edge of the surf where the water gave his muscles some support. "This feels good," he said. "You don't know what fun it would be to move a toe."

Later a friend told Franklin about a place called Warm Springs in Georgia. This was an old run-down summer resort. There was a large spring of warm water. Indians had believed this spring helped sick people get well. Even in their wars they had kept peace near the spring.

Franklin went to Warm Springs. In the warm water he could swim for hours without getting cold. This exercise helped his legs more than anything else had done. He learned to stand erect. But he had to wear braces that ran from his hips to his ankles, and use a cane. Then he learned to take a step or two. It was a proud day.

"Most of the people who have polio are children," Franklin told Eleanor.

"They need these springs most. I wish all of them could come here."

"Where would they stay?" she asked. "There are only a few old buildings. And there are no doctors to take care of patients. Besides, many children who have polio are poor. Even if they knew about the spring, those poor children could not afford to come."

"But suppose there were some kind of organization that would help?"

It was an idea that stuck in Franklin's mind. He kept thinking of the many children who suffered from polio. His sickness had made him sensitive to the troubles of others. And so with his help the Warm Springs Foundation was started. Money came in from people all over the country.

A hospital and cottages were built by the springs. In the years that followed thousands of polio patients were helped there. Many of them could never have had this treatment had it not been for Franklin Roosevelt.

The constant exercises that Franklin took made his arms and shoulders very powerful. But he would never get back the use of his legs. Except for that he was in good health. Once more he began to take part in politics. In the fall of 1928 he was nominated to run for Governor of New York.

Many people thought this was a mistake. They thought Roosevelt was still too sick to campaign. Even if he was well, they said, he was crippled. How would he get around the state?

"I'll show them!" Roosevelt told Eleanor.

By train and automobile he raced up and down the state. He made hundreds of speeches. Sometimes he had to be carried on the stage. Sometimes he was rolled on in his wheelchair. He had to hold to the speaker's stand for support when he stood up. But his voice was clear and strong. He seemed to grow healthier as the campaign went on. He was back in the fight now, and having a wonderful time.

When the votes were counted, he had won!

# Chapter 7

# Governor of New York

Governor Roosevelt traveled up and down his state to see what needed to be done. Often Eleanor went with him. Sometimes she visited places where he could not go. Then she told him about them. She was a great help in his efforts to get better wages for laborers and better conditions for women and children who needed to work. Both Franklin and Eleanor were interested in helping those who most needed help.

Roosevelt had been Governor less than one year when a depression hit the country. It came almost as suddenly as polio had struck Roosevelt. Businesses failed. This put men out of work. Without jobs they could not buy new homes or new clothes. Men who built houses were soon out of work. Men who owned stores could not sell their goods. So more businesses failed.

The longer the depression lasted the more terrible it became. It was like a snowball rolling down hill, getting bigger and bigger.

In the fall of 1930 Roosevelt was elected Governor for a second term. Now his main job was to fight the depression. But the depression was not in New York alone. It was nationwide.

Governor Roosevelt tried to make jobs for people who had lost theirs. State money was used to help feed the hungry. All over the country people stood in lines to get free bread and soup.

Television had not yet been invented. Radio too was then quite new. Roosevelt was the first politician to make much use of it. He began a series of "fireside chats." Sitting in his office he would talk over the radio to the people of his state. He would call them, "My friends," and tell what he was doing to try to end the depression.

Roosevelt had not forgotten his dream of being President. He knew that many persons blamed the Republican President, Herbert Hoover, for the great depression.

This was not fair, but it was a natural reaction. Roosevelt was sure a Democrat could be elected in 1932. But could he get the nomination?

In his fireside chats Roosevelt began to talk about the problems of the whole country as well as those of New York. He talked about better prices for farmers and jobs for people out of work. He did not know how to solve all these problems, but his warm, friendly voice made people feel he cared about them. All over the nation people began to say, "If Roosevelt becomes President, he will try to help us. He will do something to end the depression."

The Democratic Convention was held in Chicago. At home, Roosevelt and his family listened closely to their radio.

On the first ballot he had more votes than anyone else, but not enough for the nomination.

The voting went on and on. Suddenly, on the second day, California changed her votes to Roosevelt. When the news came over the radio, Roosevelt's sons began to cheer. "You've got it!"

The election was not nearly so close as the nomination. Roosevelt carried 42 of the 48 states. Now he was President-elect of the United States.

*Chapter* **8**

# President of the United States

While Roosevelt was running for President the depression got worse and worse. Banks failed and families lost all the money they had saved. Even people who still had jobs were afraid of the future. The nation was afraid.

Roosevelt took office on March 4, 1933. It was a cold, gray, windy day in Washington, but a crowd gathered in front of the Capitol. They wanted to hear the new President.

Very slowly Roosevelt came out of the Capitol building. He was helped by his tall son James, now a grown man. At last he reached the speaker's platform.

The Chief Justice of the Supreme Court read the oath of office. Roosevelt repeated it. Then he turned to face the crowd. The cold wind ruffled his hair. His voice was high and clear.

*"This is . . . the time to speak the truth, the whole truth, frankly and bluntly. Nor need we shrink from honestly facing the conditions in our country today. This great nation will endure as it has endured, will revive and prosper."*

The crowd listened without making a sound. All over America people listened to their radios.

America could grow plenty of food for its people, Roosevelt said. America could build enough houses. America could manufacture enough clothes. *"The only thing we have to fear is fear itself."*

The new government, Roosevelt said, would take quick action to put people back to work. *"This nation asks for action, and action now!"* The President's words gave America hope.

Roosevelt acted. First, he closed all the banks. He did this so no more banks would fail before laws could be passed to help them. He called Congress into special session and asked for such laws. "The house is burning down," one congressman said, "and the President of the United States says this is the way to put out the fire."

Quickly Congress passed the laws Roosevelt asked for. There was a bill to help the farmers. There was a bill to help people who were about to lose their homes. The government began what it called CCC camps. Young men in these camps planted trees, improved parks, built roads. They did not make much money, but they were working. They had food and a place to sleep.

Roosevelt kept on with his fireside chats. Over the radio he told the people what he was trying to do. He asked them to help him and Congress put an end to the depression.

People felt inspired by Roosevelt's spirit. They were no longer so afraid. They were sure their country would win the battle of the depression.

Even so, there were some who did not like the things Roosevelt was doing. These things seemed too new and strange. "Roosevelt is a radical," some people said. "He will ruin the country."

Chapter *9*

# World War II

Little by little the times got better.
Roosevelt never doubted they would. He
was always confident. He worked long
hours at a desk piled high with work.
Even the things his enemies said did
not trouble him very much.

Once a visitor asked Roosevelt how
he got so much work done. The
President threw back his big head and
laughed. "I can't move around my

office," he said, "but what advantage is there in moving around an office? I used to walk the rug in the old days, and what did I accomplish? I wore a hole in the rug." Now, Roosevelt said, still laughing, he just sat at his desk and worked.

In 1936 Roosevelt ran for a second term. This time he carried every state except Maine and Vermont. It was the greatest victory for any President in more than 100 years.

As times got better in the United States, trouble was growing in Europe. Mussolini had become dictator of Italy. Hitler had come to power in Germany. In September, 1939, England and France went to war against Germany. This was the start of World War II.

Over the radio Roosevelt talked to the American people. *"When peace has been broken anywhere, the peace of all countries everywhere is in danger."* Even so, he hoped to keep the United States out of the war. *"As long as it remains within my power . . . there will be no blackout of peace in the United States."*

Like most Americans, Roosevelt wanted the British and French to win. He helped them get supplies from the United States. He got Congress to lend the British 50 American destroyers. Yet the Germans kept winning.

Even before the war a great scientist named Albert Einstein had written Roosevelt a letter. In it he told how it might be possible to make a new and powerful bomb. This would be done

by splitting the atom. Such a thing had never been done. Many persons believed it was impossible. If it could be done, it would be the most terrible weapon ever made.

Roosevelt was not a scientist. He could not fully understand Einstein's idea. However, he called together some of America's most brilliant scientists. He showed them the letter. He put them to work in great secrecy. From their work, six years later, would come the dreadful atom bomb to end the war.

While the war was raging in Europe, Roosevelt decided to run for a third term as President. No President had ever served more than twice. Even George Washington had refused to run for a third term.

But in Europe the war was going badly. On the other side of the world Japan was at war with China. Japanese armies were threatening the Philippine Islands, owned by the United States.

Most Americans did not want to change Presidents in a time of such danger. In 1940 Franklin Roosevelt was elected for a third time.

Sunday afternoon, December 7, 1941, President Roosevelt was having lunch with his friend, Harry Hopkins, the Secretary of Commerce. The President wore an old sweater belonging to one of his sons. At 1:47 the phone rang.

"Mr. President," the White House operator said, "Secretary of the Navy Knox is calling. He insists on speaking to you right away."

"Put him on," the President said. Then, "Hello, Frank."

Knox's voice shook with excitement. *"Mr. President, it looks as if the Japanese have attacked Pearl Harbor!"*

# *Chapter* *10*

# Last Journey Home

Germany and Italy as well as Japan quickly declared war on the United States.

Now Roosevelt had a bigger job than ever before. Even before he got out of bed in the morning he was at work, reading newspapers and important letters. Government officials came and went while he dressed. He was at his desk late into the night.

Roosevelt knew, however, that to stand this strain he must keep his health. Each day he swam in the White House pool. No matter how busy, he would stop now and then to play with his little black dog named Fala. Sometimes he would go for a cruise on the Potomac River.

As President, Roosevelt was the commander in chief of the Army and Navy. Almost every day there were important decisions that only he could make. These decisions would affect the whole course of the war.

He had to decide how many ships and planes and tanks our factories would try to build.

He had to decide how many men would be in the Army and Navy.

He had to choose the admirals and generals who would lead them.

England, China and Russia were allies of the United States. The English leader was named Winston Churchill. Together, he and Roosevelt decided we would first try to win the war in Europe. Then all the allies would attack the Japanese.

Churchill met with Roosevelt a number of times to make these plans. They liked each other at once.

"Meeting him is like opening a bottle of champagne," Churchill said.

And Roosevelt told Churchill, "It is fun being in the same decade with you."

Often they talked together until late at night. This worried Mrs. Roosevelt, who scolded them for losing sleep.

Their friendship was important. It helped the generals and the armies of both countries to work together.

At first the war went badly. But slowly things began to change. New ships were built to join the Navy. On a South Pacific island called Guadalcanal, the U. S. Marines stopped the Japanese advance. In Europe, British and American soldiers invaded Italy.

In the United States, 1944 was an election year. Roosevelt had now been President twelve years. He had seen his country through a great depression. He had seen it through three years of war. Despite his great energy he was tired. To the Chairman of the Democratic Party Roosevelt wrote: *"All that is within me cries out to go back to my home on the Hudson River.*" But the country was still in danger. He would serve once more as President, if the people wanted him.

The people elected him to a fourth term—the only President to be elected more than twice!

There was still the war to be won. But now Roosevelt was thinking about the kind of world we would have after the war. He and Churchill went to Yalta, in Russia, to meet with Joseph Stalin, the Russian leader. Together they made plans for the United Nations. This was Roosevelt's great dream. He wanted a world where all the nations would work together for peace.

After the Yalta Conference, Roosevelt reported to Congress what he had done.

As he talked his voice was tired. He looked tired. But suddenly his famous smile would flash. Then he would look strong again.

In late March, Roosevelt went to Warm Springs to rest. Now his face was gray and thin. On April 12, 1945, he was sitting in his wheelchair before the fireplace. An artist was painting his picture. While she worked he looked at some new stamps in his collection. But soon he put these aside and turned to his work.

Suddenly he put one hand to his head as though it hurt. He fell back in his chair. In a little while he was dead.

All over the world people were shocked. Soldiers in Europe stopped and stared at one another. On ships in the

Pacific men cried without shame. In Washington, in towns all across America, the people mourned.

Roosevelt's body was taken back to Washington. There was a brief, simple ceremony at the White House. After that came the final trip home to Hyde Park. Under the big trees where once he had built his make-believe ship, Franklin Roosevelt was buried.